For Your Garden

VINES AND CLIMBERS

For Your Garden

VINES AND CLIMBERS

WARREN SCHULTZ

FRIEDMAN/FAIRFAX
PUBLISHERS

A FRIEDMAN/FAIRFAX BOOK

Library of Congress Cataloging-in-Publication Data

Schultz, Warren.
  Vines and climbers / Warren Schultz.
      p. cm. — (For your garden)
  Includes index.
  ISBN 1-56799-276-5 (pbk.)
  1. Ornamental climbing plants. I. Title. II. Series.
SB427.S38 1996
635.9'74—dc20   95-52702
                                                   CIP

Editor: Stephen Slaybaugh
Art Directors: Jeff Batzli and Lynne Yeamans
Layout: Robbi Oppermann Firestone
Photography Editor: Colleen Branigan

Color separations by Fine Arts Repro House Co., Ltd.
Printed in China by Leefung-Asco Printers Ltd.

For bulk purchases and special sales, please contact:
Friedman/Fairfax Publishers
Attention: Sales Department
15 West 26th Street
New York, NY 10010
(212) 685-6610 FAX (212) 685-1307

Website: http: //www.webcom.com/friedman/

Table of Contents

INTRODUCTION

*M*ystery. Maturity. Opulence, abundance, and adventure. Vines and climbers can bring many moods to a landscape. These creeping, crawling, climbing, twining plants can give a garden new dimensions by adding height, depth, and romance.

Vines and climbers can serve as the backbone of a garden by adding structure to a developing landscape or revitalizing an older one.

Vines can be humble and undemanding, growing in the background and fulfilling the role of a framework for favorite plants. Or they can serve as featured plants by covering a trellis or arbor with fascinating foliage or beautiful blooms.

They can divide a landscape into outdoor rooms, giving special areas a feeeling of intimacy. Providing shade faster than a tree, covering ground more rapidly than grass, vines can also fill a space while you're waiting for slower plants to come into their own.

Vines and climbers seem to burst with energy. You can almost feel their inexorable growth as soon as you enter a garden where they live. Vines bring a sense of motion to the garden. They seem to spring to life as soon as they hit the ground, and always convey a feeling of growth barely under control.

So much of our gardening is done at ground level: we bend and stoop and crawl. Vines and climbers direct our vision upward; their foliage being at the gardener's eye level. When you're ready to move beyond simple beds and borders, it's time to move up to vines.

OPPOSITE: Climbers have their own seasons of glory in the sun. *Vitis Coignetiae* comes alive in streaming sunlight and, here, frames a fountain in a formal scene.

ABOVE: Sometimes vines are most valuable when they stretch out rather than up. Here, vinca serves as a backdrop to highlight a bright red azalea. The green carpet helps to knit the flowering plant to the stone path.

LEFT: When a light hand is called for, vines may be used to mimic or enhance natural conditions. This soft blanket of running cedar surrounding the base of a tree presents a clean, weedless look without seeming artificial.

ABOVE: Climbers need not be massive and intrusive to make a statement. Here, a simple vine wreath against a weathered fence creates a decorative addition.

OPPOSITE: Roses are at the top of most gardeners' lists of favorite climbing plants. At some point, nearly every gardener has dreamed of a rose-covered cottage. Here, rambling over the roof and sides of the cottage, the flowers perfume the air with their sweet fragrance.

LEFT: Mystery hangs like warm, thick air in this garden corner, where the light is softened by a profusion of vines both above and below. These vines serve to frame the formal fountain and focus attention on it.

OPPOSITE: Sometimes vines are asked to remain in the background and faithfully serve as accompaniment to surrounding garden plants and features. This trellis seems to be awaiting the growth of a vine, perhaps from the ivy climbing the nearby tree, adding a sense of expectation to the garden scene.

OPPOSITE: Gardeners often think of German ivy as a green screen that's easily ignored as it fades into the background. But in autumn, the ivy bursts into color. An awareness of the changing faces of vines and a readiness to combine them with surrounding colors allows the observant designer to create an eye-catching scene.

ABOVE: Some vines, such as wisteria, are coveted for their color. The spare architectural form of the vine and the airy clouds of bloom are light enough to let hardscape accents, like this window frame, shine through. Even unlikely color combinations work well with wisteria.

ABOVE: Light, airy, old-fashioned, and just plain pretty, sweet peas and runner beans on a trellis provide a focal point for the vegetable garden, giving it a more unique quality.

OPPOSITE: Like bright raindrops dripping down a wall, these vines add a sense of movement to the scene and draw the eye to the trough of alpine plants on the ground.

ABOVE: Virginia creeper and buttercup ivy have been given free rein to grow wild, bringing a feeling of age and enchantment to a corner of the garden. It may be for only a small spot in a new garden, but ivy, coupled with the artful placement of a garden artifact, adds a feeling of depth to the scene.

ABOVE: Tracing the outline of this wooden fence, these nasturtiums seem ready to embrace anyone who cares to stop and rest on the stone bench.

OPPOSITE: In the limited space of an urban patio, the vertical quality of vines provides the ability to create an interesting arrangement. The pot of 'Carnival de Nice' tulips adds a splash of color to the green backdrop. This composition, framed by the variegated leaves of the vine draped over the wall, can be enjoyed indoors or out.

ABOVE: Hanging like jewels from a bracelet, golden laburnum and purple wisteria add height and depth to this garden bed.

OPPOSITE: Some vining plants, such as wisteria, can be trained as standards that do not need any support. They add a sense of seclusion to the surrounding garden.

Chapter One

DESIGNING WITH VINES AND CLIMBERS

*S*ooner or later, faced with a bare wall, a boring lawn, or a young garden that's slow to mature, every gardener recognizes the appeal of vines and climbers. They're among the most versatile of all garden plants. It would be difficult to find another plant that would work as hard or as fast to transform a landscape.

Vines and climbers can match any mood you wish to create in the garden. The dignified and stately look of an ivy-covered hall or the bright and cheery country feel of morning glories on a garden fence are just two examples of the effective uses of vines.

When considering the look you desire for your garden, give a little thought to vines. Do you need a vertical accent or a splash of color to draw the eye? You might desire an arbor covered with clematis. Do you need to soften a fence that surrounds a vegetable garden? Sow morning glories or nasturtiums. Is your lawn growing old and hard to maintain? Consider a lamium or pachysandra corner to reduce the size of your lawn. Perhaps you want to create a secluded, mysterious spot in the corner of the garden. Ivy will do the trick quickly.

Always keep in mind the effect you're after. If you want an airy, bright feel, use annual flowering vines. To extend the garden season, choose evergreen perennial vines. Or try combining a few different vines. Whatever you choose, you're sure to find that your garden can be improved by adding the vertical accents of vines and climbers.

OPPOSITE: An arbor at a lawn's edge is an inviting spot to stop and survey the garden. These informal, fast-growing hops spilling over the arbor provide a natural, untamed feeling, matching the catmint planting below.

ABOVE: A wooden door and an adobe wall may seem stark and uninviting, but as ivy crawls over the hard surface, it softens the scene and makes the entry seem more approachable.

ABOVE: Climbers and creepers can be combined in a landscape for a lush effect. Billowing jasmine on an arbor seems to rise on the horizon like a cloud from a sea of green ivy.

RIGHT: All too often patios are overexposed and thus seem uninviting. A simple arbor of roses provides a sense of security and enclosure to this space, making it a more welcoming place to spend a summer afternoon.

OPPOSITE: Sometimes slight and delicate vines, such as these runner beans, are the perfect touch. Here, they allow the beauty of the trellis to show through.

OPPOSITE: It's a rare landscape that entices the visitor to look up; so much of our time in the garden is spent gazing downward. Plants that guide our vision and our spirits upward, such as this wisteria on a pergola, feel especially refreshing and rich.

LEFT: Getting the most from vines requires planning and some patience. Consider the structure and material that the plant will grow against. Do you want contrast or harmony? A white blooming hydrangea goes well with most supporting colors. Pruned sparingly, it can't help but be noticed and appreciated.

ABOVE: Gardens, especially new ones, can sometimes seem too flat and one-dimensional. But an arbor covered with a fast-growing vine, such as clematis, offers an entirely new dimension.

ABOVE: With its supple stems, ivy can be trained to take the shape of any garden and its accents. This vine will eagerly grow to cover a sphere with just a bit of tending.

RIGHT: Color is key to any garden. Sometimes subdued shades are called for. At other times and in other places, brighter and bolder colors are better. A blazing trumpet vine calls attention to this courtyard.

OPPOSITE: An entryway is the first place that a vine can make an impact. The first decision for the gardener is whether to choose a vine that climbs or trails. Even in the dark, the scent of this trailing jasmine will draw the visitor to the gate.

ABOVE: Repetition and rhythm are easily incorporated when designing with vines. Elegant climbing roses frame a simple door; the pattern is then repeated on the window beside it.

RIGHT: Climbing plants can add a sense of order to lush and jumbled plantings. Standing like bookends, these roses frame the plantings and draw the eye upward. At the same time, they're trained to conform to the pattern on the brick wall.

ABOVE: When it comes to climbing plants, there are few that are as versatile and as full of feeling as roses. Old-fashioned climbers can add a dash of color to a rustic scene. Even if they're newly planted, they bring to mind abandoned wild plantings.

RIGHT: A bower of wisteria can punctuate a garden path and provide a welcome relief from the summer sun.

LEFT: Vibrant when in full bloom, jasmine seems to take on many new qualities. Here, it appears as a welcoming guest at this patio table where the vine's sweet scent perfumes the air.

ABOVE: English ivy is often used as a rampant cover, left to grow eagerly over all it encounters. For a more elegant look, keep ivy's growth in check with careful pruning, and it will follow and echo the shape of a trellis or arbor.

ABOVE: Width and breadth are as important as height when designing with vines. Here, roses are kept within boundaries to remain in the same scale as the bench—and perfume without being overwhelming. Visitors who stop to rest here will be embraced by the roses' beauty.

LEFT: Sometimes a simple coverlet of green is all that's called for. Ivy adds a sense of enchantment to the corner of this garden.

ABOVE: We often think of ivy as a mass, a plant best left to cover vast, blank areas. But it can also serve as a rich green accent in an off-season window box.

ABOVE: Even when ivy is put to work on a common task, such as covering a brick wall, its effect can be heightened by such accessories as these delicate shutters and simple window box.

RIGHT: Clematis is a garden favorite, renowned for its abundant, rich blooms, delicate foliage, and genteel climbing habits. Light and airy, it's best used to emphasize the frame on which it grows.

Chapter Two

PROBLEM-SOLVING VINES

We use flowers, shrubs, and trees as bright splashes of paint on our landscape canvases. We may plant and feed and fuss over them, but they are only a small part of the picture. For best presentation they need only a well-thought-out background. But too often the space around and between annuals and perennials is blank canvas, most likely a long, dull stretch of labor-intensive lawn. Creeping ground covers can add a more exciting texture and tone to the overall picture.

Vines don't have to grow upward to enhance a yard. Sometimes their horizontal nature is just as welcome in a garden. There are many vines that are at their best when they're allowed room to roam. Planted in corners, they'll soften the edges of the lawn. They can also provide a transition between that patch of grass and more wild areas. Grown around a deck, vines can impart a look that turf cannot.

Versatile ground covers bring many looks to a landscape. They can be as well behaved and understated as pachysandra or as stately as ivy. They can be as wild as honeysuckle, evoking the feeling of an abandoned estate.

Creeping vines are, as a rule, undemanding. Growing thick and running fast and far, they require little care.

OPPOSITE: Bright yellow creeping Jenny finds a more subdued mate in the pink-flowered sedum. Together they blanket the ground with color, which will last throughout the season.

ABOVE: As vigorous as a weed, Hall's honeysuckle will climb, creep, and trail as long as it is allowed. It can be used to cover ground, structures, or any material that's best hidden.

ABOVE: What do you turn to when you need cover in a hurry? The common morning glory. Nothing grows faster to form a deep carpet of fresh green foliage. And nothing compares to its cheery blooms, either.

RIGHT: A rampant grower, honeysuckle will cover everything in its path, forming a thicket that smothers weeds. The variety 'Dropmore Scarlet' is favored for its bright red flowers that persist from early summer into late autumn.

ABOVE: It grows fast to cover the ground in great waves of white-spotted dark green leaves. It erupts into blue flowers that fade to pink. It thrives north or south, in sunlight or light shade. All these characteristics make Bethlehem sage one of the best ground covers around.

ABOVE: There's no ground cover more common than pachysandra, but freed from its usual placement—in the circle surrounding the base of a tree—and left to roam over an expansive area, pachysandra can add an element of elegance to the landscape.

RIGHT: Sometimes a mound of flowers is the key to a successful landscape. Abundant with blooms, clematis can easily fill that role.

OPPOSITE: A ground cover need not exist only as a uniform sea of green. Mixing plants adds interest and excitement. Here, saxifrage, lamium, and euphorbia are combined for a striking effect.

OPPOSITE: Woodbine, with its stately stems and refined foliage, is a good choice to cover gates, fences, and walls. It takes on an interesting look through the seasons as small green flowers give way to dark berries and bright autumn foliage.

LEFT: Some ground covers are made for the shade. Lamium, with its silver leaves and clusters of delicate flowers, prefers to grow where the soil is moist and the sunlight is dim.

ABOVE: Versatility is one of the strengths of common ivy. Gardeners can use it in many different ways, such as allowing it to creep and flow down a set of stone steps.

LEFT: Climbing roses grow fast and bloom profusely, and many offer a delightful scent, making them a perfect choice for covering walls and fences.

OPPOSITE: It's sometimes hard to understand the obscurity of porcelain *Ampelopsis.* This deciduous perennial grows fast and strong with handsome bright leaves and makes a good arbor ornament. In late summer and autumn, it produces clusters of bird-attracting berries of many colors.

LEFT: The bright bark of a eucalyptus tree seems even richer when contrasted with a climbing blanket of ivy. The vine also serves to keep the ground free of weeds and undesirable plants.

OPPOSITE: A planter filled with bright annuals could be lost against a plain brick background. But a wall of ivy plays the perfect supporting role, allowing the flowering plants to shine.

Chapter Three

FAST EFFECTS WITH ANNUAL VINES AND CLIMBERS

*T*hey may not grow quite as fast as Jack's beanstalk, but annual vines can make fast magic in the landscape. Sown in spring, the plants seem to burst from the soil and climb upward without pause. In the process they'll quickly transform a garden spot with their lush foliage and vibrant blooms.

Does your vegetable garden seem a bit dull? A few bright-flowered ornamental beans clambering up a tepee will take care of that. Want to dress up that front fence? A few morning glories twining through the pickets will transform the scene. Waiting for shrubs, trees, or a hedge to fill in? You can put annual vines to work as part-time scene stealers.

In just a weekend you can begin a new look for a garden spot. Erect a simple trellis and sow a few seeds, and you're on your way to a new dimension in gardening.

Annual vines and climbers are growth personified. These simple, unassuming plants convey their own special playfulness and free nature. Covering walls and fences or climbing up trellises, they speak of sunny summer days, bright cottage gardens, and country farmhouses.

OPPOSITE: If provided with a foothold, nasturtiums will climb by twisting their leaf stems around a trellis, fence, wire, or wall. The edible flowers add a peppery flavor to salads.

ABOVE: It's hard to beat nasturtiums for fast cover and rich colors. The plants bring an old-fashioned look to the edge of a flower or vegetable garden that never goes out of favor.

LEFT: Known as clock vine for its bright, orange faces, *Thunbergia* brings a lush tropical look to a hanging planter, window box, or garden bed. This Mexican native grows fast from seed and thrives in the sun.

ABOVE: Vegetables that are equally at home in the flower garden or clambering up a porch post, scarlet runner beans offer rich, bright colors on delicate, quick-twining vines.

ABOVE: It may be their deep, pure colors of violet, white, and pink, or perhaps it's their petals' velvety look or fresh green leaves. Maybe it's the speed with which they grow, or the memories of simple gardens they inspire. Whatever the reason, morning glories never go out of fashion as a climbing vine for a fence or post.

RIGHT: Morning glory vines may reach up to ten feet (3m) in length in a single season. Just sow them in place in a sunny location and they'll find a way to climb into the spotlight.

ABOVE: The common nasturtium has an exotic relative that's rarely seen in gardens: the canary creeper. Though its flowers are smaller and always bright yellow, its foliage is more intriguing than that of the common nasturtium. It climbs more readily as well.

RIGHT: One of the best ways to beautify a vegetable planting is with a tepee of runner beans. The variety 'White Achievement' grows into a solid mass of foliage and blooms with delightful white flowers in midsummer.

OPPOSITE: Hops are bound to attract attention and inspire comments from garden visitors. These rampant growers produce intriguing seed pods from which beer is made.

OPPOSITE: Flame flower is another nasturtium relative and has electrifying red blooms. Though perennial in warm areas, it's often grown as an annual where the weather is cool.

ABOVE: The cup and saucer vine offers large purple and green or white flowers on a fast-growing vine that may reach up to twenty-five feet (7.6m) in a single season. This Mexican native can be sown in a sunny location and allowed to climb over a fence or trellis.

RIGHT: When the talk is of charming, old-fashioned flowers, sweet peas usually head the list. They're known for their wide variety of colors and delightful fragrance.

Chapter Four

PERMANENCE FROM PERENNIAL VINES

*P*erennial vines and climbers add permanence and stateliness to the landscape. With their strong forms, rich textures, and elegant blooms, perennial vines can enliven a wall or an arbor. Above all else, they convey the feeling of energetic growth. Indeed, they make a landscape come alive with their ambition. Covering a wall or climbing relentlessly up an arbor or a pergola, they seem to say that nature will not be subdued.

A garden can be built around perennial vines and climbers. If you plant them in a good spot, they'll be there from year to year, adding their own elegant tone to the garden. Many offer exotic flowers in deep colors and appealing shapes. Others remain attractive through all four seasons, offering autumn color or having bright green foliage through the bleak winter months.

The features of perennial vines are nearly endless. Many provide exotic flowers that attract butterflies and hummingbirds, or grow gnarled strong trunks that offer shelter to birds.

Perennial vines are perfect for hefty arbors, classic pergolas, porches, and walls. These climbers can hold their own against large structures, reducing the hardscape of the landscape to an appealing scale.

OPPOSITE: Wisteria provides a touch of southern elegance far into northern areas. The rich purple or white flowers appear early in spring, releasing their seductive fragrance far and wide.

ABOVE: At first glance you might not guess that actinidia is a close relative of the plant that bears kiwi fruit. This ornamental kiwi unfurls its leaves in spring with an unlikely combination of white, pink, and green. If both male and female plants are present, they will also produce small, edible fruit.

ABOVE: Five-leaf akebia offers nearly everything a gardener could want. Its woody vines, covered with delicate foliage, produce sweet-smelling flowers in spring. It can also find a place in the food garden as it grows smalls clusters of handsome edible fruit. Growing to thirty feet (9.1m), akebia can be planted to climb a trellis or ramble over the ground.

RIGHT: Star jasmine is tougher than it looks. Its delicate white flowers and delightful scent belie its aggressive nature and tough demeanor. It's a good choice for covering banks and clambering up walls.

OPPOSITE: Clematis is often the first choice for a perennial climber, and a good choice it is. This herbaceous vine grows rapidly in spring from a moist, shady site, with large, luxurious blooms exploding into the sunlight. Clematis will climb a lamppost, cover a roof, or spread over a bank without fuss.

OPPOSITE: The crimson glory vine, a common grape relative, is at its best in autumn. That's when the foliage turns a fiery red and lights up the landscape.

LEFT: Ivy is the strong, silent type in the landscape. It grows fast and does all that is required without complaint. Ivy is often over-looked, but variegated varieties such as *Hedera colchica* 'Sulpherheart' are more noticeable.

ABOVE: A single purple wisteria flower cluster, reaching up to twenty inches (50.8cm) in length, is a thing of beauty in itself. A mature vine covered with blooms can take one's breath away.

ABOVE: An evergreen in warm areas such as Florida, the passion flower is one of the more dramatic flowering vines. Fast-growing and vigorous, the plant produces sweetly scented flowers that attract butterflies.

RIGHT: Available in many shapes, sizes, and colors, Italian clematis 'Abundance' is known for its rapid growth and delicate hanging, pinkish red flowers that appear in late summer.

ABOVE: Porcelain *Ampelopsis* is known for its bright berries of blue, green, purple, and pink. They appear in autumn on beautiful, strong plants.

OPPOSITE: Though they won't climb without assistance, roses are among the most popular choices for covering walls and fences. 'Climbing Peace' may be the most renowned of gardeners' favorites. With just a little help, these roses will gladly grow skyward.

ABOVE: Porches are where you'll normally find Dutchman's-pipe. The twining vines quickly climb any available support, while the huge, kidney-shaped leaves provide deep shade. In late spring, small, brown, pipe-shaped flowers appear.

RIGHT: Even the common grape vine can play a leading role as a climber in the ornamental garden. Its lush foliage turns a deep red as autumn approaches.

ABOVE: The foliage is the most popular characteristic of ivy. Always green, it shines in seasons long after other climbers and vines have given up the ghost. Ivy keeps the garden alive all through the year.

RIGHT: The climbing hydrangea is a stately plant in any setting. Its small, white, beautifully fragrant flowers cover the strong vines of this plant in spring and early summer.

PHOTO CREDITS

© Philip Beaurline: 7, 8 (left)

© Ken Druse: 14 (left), 44, 47, 67, 69 (left)

© John Glover: 23, 24, 25 (both), 26, 29 (both), 35 (top), 45 (left), 54, 57, 61, 62 (both), 64, 66 (right), 69 (right), 70–71

© Dency Kane: 41, 51, 54–55, 56 (right), 66 (left)

© image/Dennis Kruskowski: 11

© Charles Mann: 8 (right), 9, 10, 13, 20, 21, 22 (right), 26–27, 28, 32–33, 34, 36–37, 42 (bottom), 65 (left)

© Clive Nichols: 2, 6, 12, 14 (right), 15, 16, 17, 18, 19, 38, 43, 49, 50, 56 (left), 58, 59 (both), 60, 70

© Jerry Pavia: 22 (left), 30, 33, 35 (bottom), 36, 42 (top), 45 (right), 46, 48, 53, 63, 65 (right), 68

© Richard Shiell: 30–31, 39, 40 (both), 52–53